GEOGRAPHUNNY

A Book of Global Riddles

Written and Illustrated by
MORT GERBERG

Clarion Books · New York

Library of Congress Cataloging-in-Publication Data
Gerberg, Mort.
Geographunny : a book of global riddles / written and illustrated
by Mort Gerberg.
p.   cm.
Summary: A collection of riddles about geographic names, including
"Why would you wear lots of sweaters in a certain South American
country? Because it's Chile."
ISBN 0-395-52449-0
1. Geographical recreations—Juvenile literature.   2. Riddles—
Juvenile literature.   3. Word games—Juvenile literature.
(1. Names, Geographical—Wit and humor.   2. Riddles.)   I. Title.
GV1485.G47   1991
910'.207—dc20   90-40388   CIP   AC

Clarion Books
a Houghton Mifflin Company imprint
215 Park Avenue South, New York, NY 10003
Text and Illustrations copyright © 1991 by Mort Gerberg
All rights reserved.
For information about permission to reproduce
selections from this book write to Permissions,
Houghton Mifflin Company, 2 Park Street, Boston, MA 02108.
Printed in the USA.

The artwork in this book was prepared in pen and ink with
watercolor dyes.

WOZ 10 9 8 7 6 5 4 3 2 1

For Eva Rachel Jaffe, whose riddle
gave me the idea to do this book,
and for Lilia Anya Gerberg, who makes me smile
all throughout the world.

How to Riddle Your Way Through This Book

Riddles are questions that are word puzzles. In *Geographunny*, the answers to the riddles all have something to do with geography. There are hints in the pictures, and there are maps to help with the solutions, too. Many of the riddles and their answers are humorous plays on words that sound the same or nearly the same, but mean something different. This kind of wordplay is called a pun. The best way to riddle your way through *Geographunny* is to read out loud, because you may hear the answer before you actually think of it. The "overheard conversations" on pages 21, 35, 49, and 63 *must* be read aloud for you to enjoy the puns fully. Should all else fail, there are answers on page 64.

Contents

1
North America

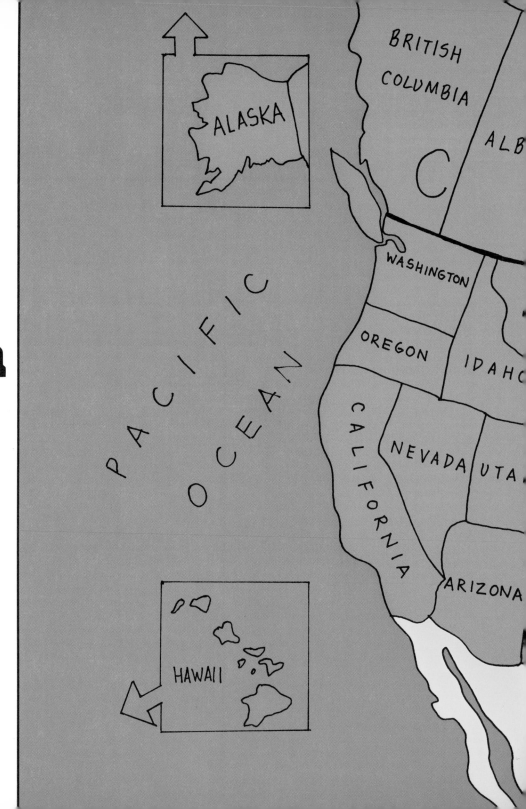

ALASKA

BRITISH
COLUMBIA

ALB

C

WASHINGTON

OREGON

IDAHO

PACIFIC

OCEAN

CALIFORNIA

NEVADA

UTA

ARIZONA

HAWAII

NORTHWEST TERR.

HUDSON BAY

SASKATCHEWAN MANITOBA ONTARIO QUEBEC

N   A   D   A

NEW BRUNSWICK

NOVA SCOTIA

TANA NORTH DAKOTA MINNESOTA LAKE SUPERIOR MAINE

MICH LAKE HURON VT NH

OMING SOUTH DAKOTA WISCONSIN IGAN TORONTO MASS

LAKE ONTARIO CONN

NEBRASKA IOWA LAKE MICHIGAN KALAMAZOO LAKE ERIE NEW YORK

LORADO ILLINOIS INDIANA OHIO PENN NJ

KANSAS MISSOURI WEST VIRGINIA MD. DELAWARE

KENTUCKY VIRGINIA

MEXICO OKLAHOMA TENNESSEE NORTH CAROLINA

ARKANSAS SOUTH CAROLINA

MISSISSIPPI ALABAMA GEORGIA

TEXAS ATLANTIC OCEAN

LOUISIANA FLORIDA

9

Which state is this a picture of?

Which southern state watches a game that is played with a racquet, a ball, and a net?

Which southern state has four eyes but can't see?

In which province of Canada would you
throw a baseball around with your friends?

Which city in Canada sounds like the name of the Lone Ranger's Native American friend?

In which northwestern state would you be
most likely to take a bath?

Which New England state is most useful to you if you have bubble gum?

Which middle western state would you like to drink?

Which state is this a picture of?

In what city in the state of Michigan would you find a gathering of wild animals?

Overheard conversation at a party for the United States: (Read aloud.)

OHIO!

IOWA DOLLAR FOR THE ICE CREAM.

KENTUCKY COME TONIGHT, BROTHER?

YES, SHE KANSAS.

I WONDER, WHAT WILL DELAWARE?

IDAHO, BUT ALASKA.

REMEMBER, JOSEPH WORE DAKOTA MANY COLORS.

THE STEREO ISN'T PLAYING. ARE ALL THE WIRES CONNECTICUT?

YES, BUT THE MAINE FUSE BLEW.

LET'S GO— THERE'S NO MORE CAKE. IT'S OREGON.

2

South of the Border

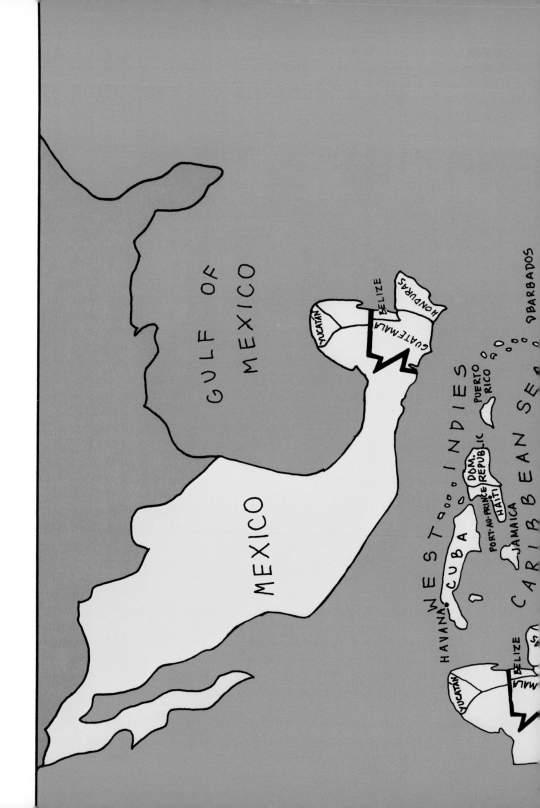

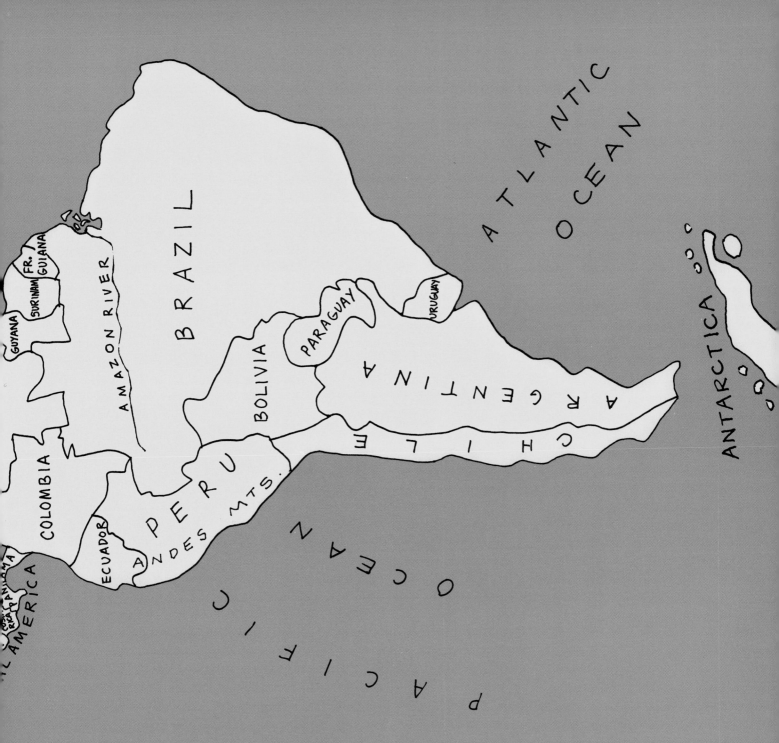

ATLANTIC OCEAN

ANTARCTICA

BRAZIL

AMAZON RIVER

GUYANA

SURINAM

FR. GUIANA

COLOMBIA

PANAMA

CENTRAL AMERICA

ECUADOR

PERU

ANDES MTS.

BOLIVIA

PARAGUAY

URUGUAY

ARGENTINA

CHILE

PACIFIC OCEAN

23

Why would you wear lots of sweaters in a certain South American country?

Which continent has ants in it?

Which island country in the Caribbean is a shape in which sugar often comes?

Which city on the coast of Peru is the name of a kind of bean?

What is this a picture of?

(It's a large body of water south of the United States.)

Which island in the West Indies reminds you of the person who cuts your hair?

Where in Mexico is sunbathing most natural?

What body of water east of Central America has a small vegetable in it?

In which country in Central America
and which island in the West Indies
will you find your parents?

Which harbor city in the West Indies is especially for the son of a king?

Overheard conversation at a party south of the border: (Read aloud.)

3
Across the Atlantic

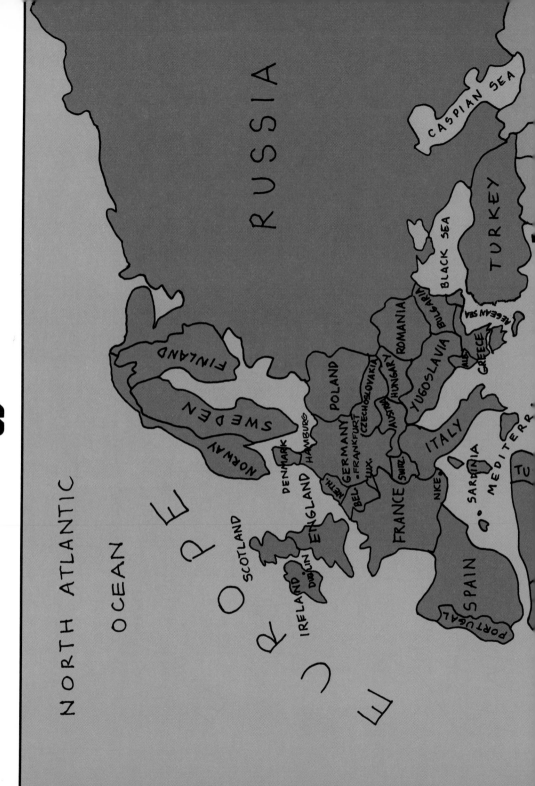

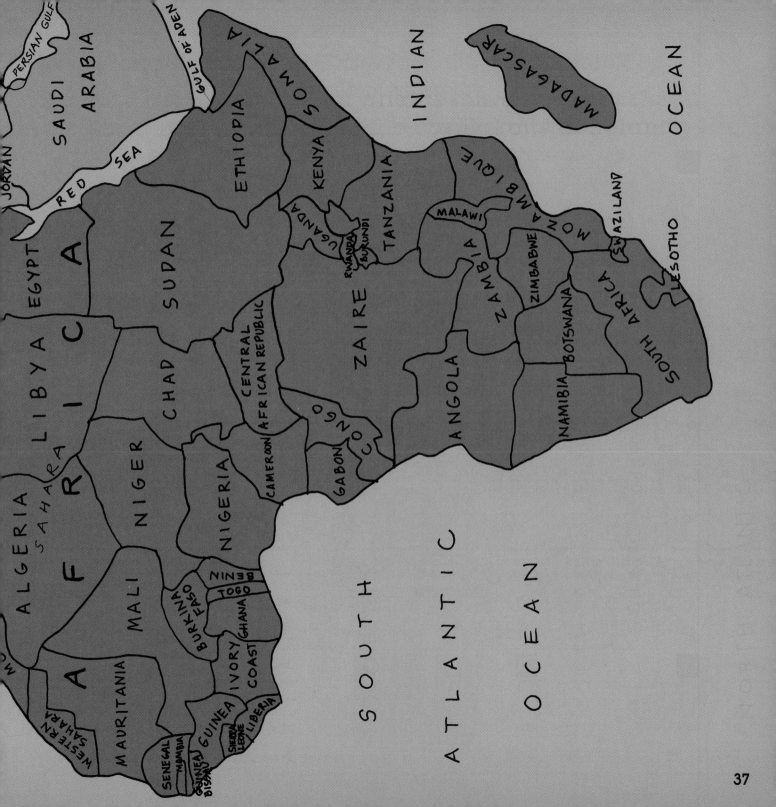

SAUDI ARABIA

PERSIAN GULF

JORDAN

GULF OF ADEN

SOMALIA

INDIAN OCEAN

MADAGASCAR

RED SEA

ETHIOPIA

KENYA

TANZANIA

MOZAMBIQUE

SWAZILAND

LESOTHO

EGYPT

SUDAN

UGANDA

RWANDA

BURUNDI

ZAIRE

MALAWI

ZAMBIA

ZIMBABWE

BOTSWANA

SOUTH AFRICA

LIBYA

CHAD

CENTRAL AFRICAN REPUBLIC

CONGO

ANGOLA

NAMIBIA

SAHARA

AFRICA

ALGERIA

NIGER

NIGERIA

CAMEROON

GABON

MALI

BENIN

TOGO

GHANA

IVORY COAST

MAURITANIA

BURKINA FASO

SOUTH

ATLANTIC

OCEAN

OCEAN

WESTERN SAHARA

SENEGAL

GAMBIA

GUINEA BISSAU

GUINEA

SIERRA LEONE

LIBERIA

MOROCCO

Which country in eastern Europe is gobbled up by others?

In which large country in eastern Europe are people always in a hurry?

What is this a picture of?
(It's the capital city of Ireland.)

0 2 4 8 16 32 64

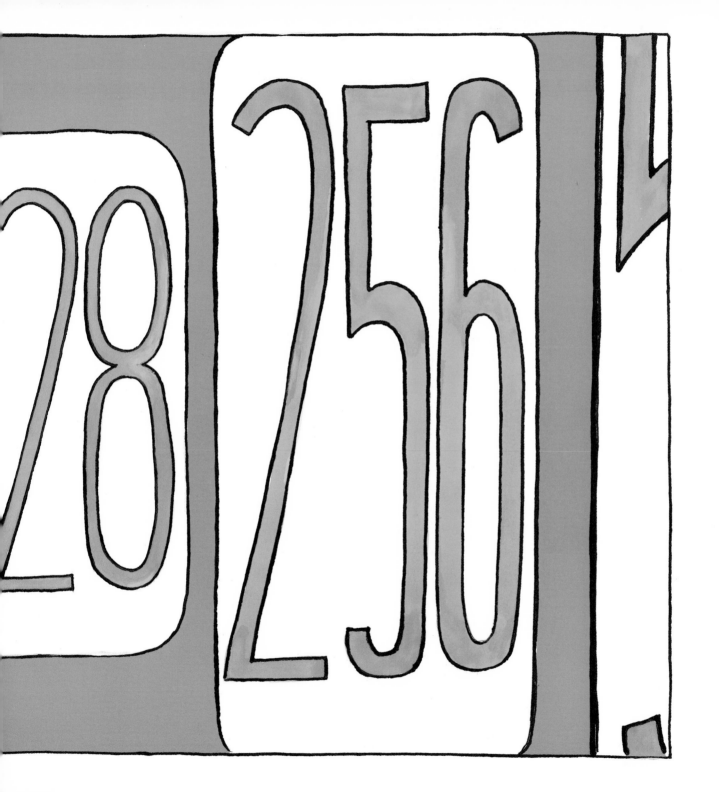

What do you do when you put syrup on pancakes?
(It's the name of a country in northern Europe.)

Which city in the south of France is especially pleasant to be in?

Which eastern European country is how you feel at noon if you didn't eat breakfast?

Which continent do you really need to have at a rodeo?

From which large Mediterranean island could you make sandwiches?

Which two cities in Germany would you eat at a ball game?

This country on the Aegean Sea is often found on wheels. What is it?

Overheard conversation at an African/Middle Eastern party: (Read aloud.)

KENYA TELL ME WHAT KIND OF A DRINK THIS IS ?

SURE. IT'S A MALTA MILKSHAKE.

SAHARA YOU BEEN ?

PRETTY GOOD. COME, SUDAN AND TALK WITH ME.

ISRAEL ? HE DOESN'T LOOK WELL AT ALL.

THE NERVE OF THAT CABBIE— EGYPT ME !

YOU'RE JOKING. OR ARE YOU SYRIA ?

4

Across the Pacific

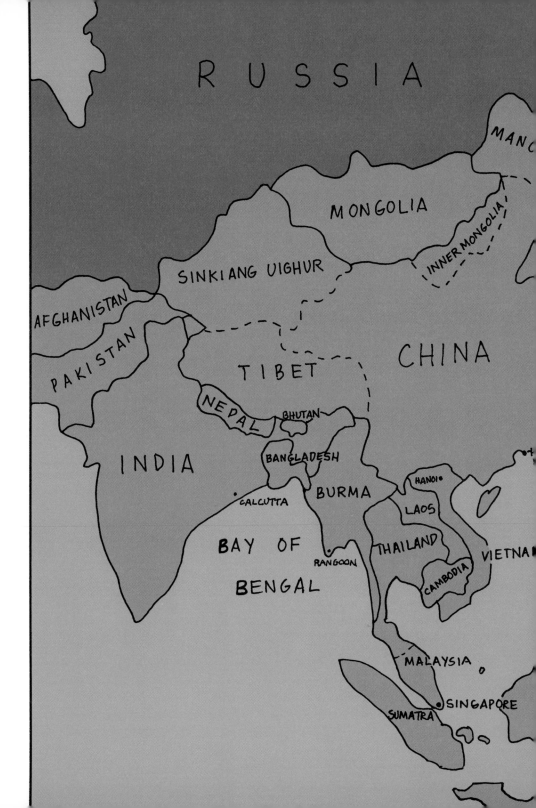

RUSSIA

MANC

MONGOLIA

INNER MONGOLIA

SINKIANG UIGHUR

AFGHANISTAN

PAKISTAN

TIBET

CHINA

NEPAL

BHUTAN

INDIA

BANGLADESH

CALCUTTA

BURMA

HANOI

LAOS

BAY OF BENGAL

RANGOON

THAILAND

VIETNA

CAMBODIA

MALAYSIA

SINGAPORE

SUMATRA

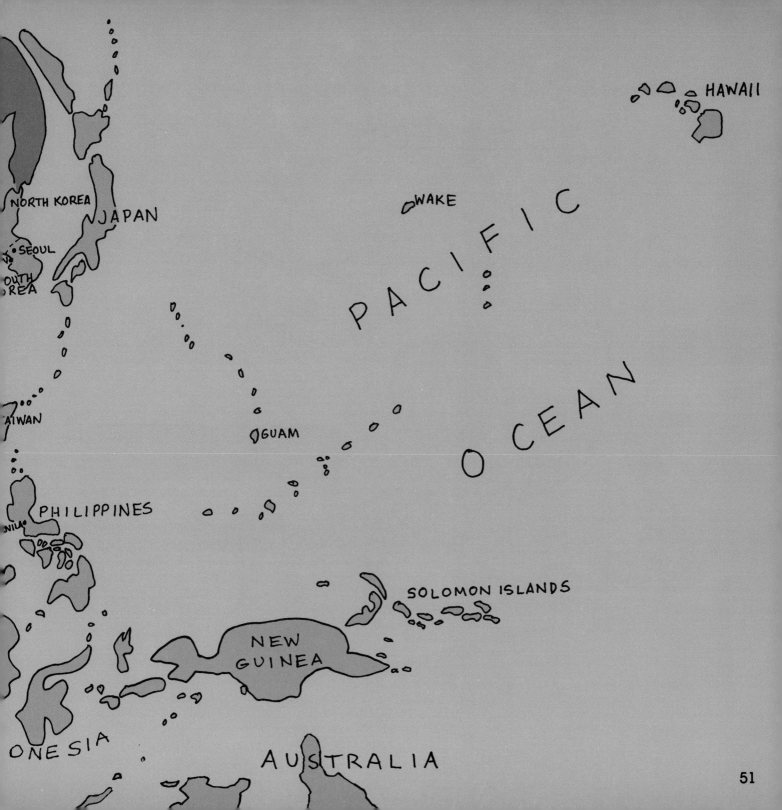

HAWAII

NORTH KOREA JAPAN

SEOUL

OUTH
OREA

WAKE

PACIFIC

TAIWAN

GUAM

OCEAN

PHILIPPINES

NILA

SOLOMON ISLANDS

NEW
GUINEA

ONESIA

AUSTRALIA

What is this a picture of?
(It's an island in the middle of the Pacific Ocean.)

Which group of islands in the South Pacific has the same name as an ancient and very wise king?

Which city in the Philippine Islands sounds like a popular ice cream flavor?

What city in China is a cousin of this world-famous gorilla?

What would you say to this Malaysian city if it didn't know the melody or words to any popular songs?
"You—————!"

Which is the teeniest tiniest city in Korea?

In which Asian country do you automatically find a utensil used to fry food?

Which city in Indonesia is what you push
around in a supermarket?

In which city in the south of Burma do you find the sound of yesterday's telephone call?

What island in Malaysia is what you are when you enter the world?

Overheard conversation at an Asian/Pacific party: (Read aloud.)

HELLO, HAWAII !

IF HE'D WANTED TO, CALCUTTA COME HERE EARLIER.

SAY, THAT'S A PRETTY TAIWAN.

THANKS, JUANITA— WANT A STICK OF CHEWING GUAM ?

FRANKLY, I'D PREFER SOME SEOUL FOOD.

I DON'T BELIEVE YOU. YOU'RE PHILIPPINES.

AND YOU'RE BEGINNING TO HANOI ME.

Answers

1. North America

11. Idaho
12. Tennessee
13. Mississippi
14. Saskatchewan
15. Toronto
16. Washington
17. Massachusetts
18. Minnesota
19. Illinois (but the s is not pronounced when you refer to the state)
20. Kalamazoo

2. South of the Border

24. Because it's Chile (chilly)
25. Antarctica
26. Cuba
27. Lima (but the city is pronounced *LEE-ma*)
28. Gulf of Mexico
30. Barbados
31. Yucatán
32. Caribbean Sea
33. Panama and Trinidad
34. Port-au-Prince

3. Across the Atlantic

38. Turkey
39. Russia
40. Dublin
42. Sweden them
43. Nice (but it is pronounced *niece*)
44. Hungary
45. Europe
46. Sardinia
47. Frankfurt and Hamburg
48. Greece

4. Across the Pacific

52. Wake
53. The Solomon Islands
54. Manila
56. Hong Kong
57. Singapore
58. Inchon
59. Japan
60. Djakarta
61. Rangoon
62. Borneo